Food Dudes

WILLIAM WRIGLEY JR.:

Wrigley's Chewing Gum Founder

Joanne Mattern

Checkerboard
Library

An Imprint of Abdo Publishing
www.abdopublishing.com

www.abdopublishing.com

Published by Abdo Publishing, a division of ABDO, PO Box 398166, Minneapolis, Minnesota 55439. Copyright © 2015 by Abdo Consulting Group, Inc. International copyrights reserved in all countries. No part of this book may be reproduced in any form without written permission from the publisher. Checkerboard Library™ is a trademark and logo of Abdo Publishing.

Printed in the United States of America, North Mankato, Minnesota.
052014
092014

 THIS BOOK CONTAINS RECYCLED MATERIALS

Cover Photos: Corbis; Getty Images
Interior Photos: Alamy p. 18; AP Images p. 26; Corbis pp. 1, 7, 16, 23; Getty Images p. 11; iStockphoto pp. 22, 25; courtesy William Wrigley Jr. Company pp. 5, 8, 9, 10, 13, 14, 15, 17, 19, 21, 24

Series Coordinator: BreAnn Rumsch
Editors: Tamara L. Britton, BreAnn Rumsch
Art Direction & Cover Design: Neil Klinepier

Library of Congress Control Number: 2014941024

Mattern, Joanne, 1963-
  William Wrigley Jr. : Wrigley's Chewing Gum founder / Joanne Mattern.
       p. cm. -- (Food dudes)
  ISBN 978-1-62403-498-5
  1. Wrigley, William, 1861-1932--Juvenile literature. 2. Wm. Wrigley Jr. Company--History--Juvenile literature. 3. Businessmen--United States--Biography--Juvenile literature. 4. Chewing gum industry--United States--History--Juvenile literature. I. Title.
  HD9970.5.C454W756 2015
  338.7'6646--dc23
  [B]
                                        2014941024

Contents

Young William

You probably agree that chewing gum is a fun, tasty treat. However, this simple product was not always as popular as it is today. When William Wrigley Jr. started his chewing gum company, he used creative **strategies** to sell gum. Today, the William Wrigley Jr. Company brands are world famous.

On September 30, 1861, William Wrigley Jr. was born in Philadelphia, Pennsylvania. William was named for his father. His mother was Mary Ladley Wrigley. Eventually, William had seven brothers and sisters.

William's mother cared for him and the other children. She also cared for the family's home. William's father was a soap maker. In 1870, he started the Wrigley Manufacturing Company to sell his soap. The company was very successful.

William took an interest in his father's business right away. So in 1871, his father let him help sell soap from a basket. William sold a lot of Wrigley's Mineral Scouring Soap on the streets of Philadelphia.

William Wrigley Jr. found success through creatively advertising his products.

Working Boy

While growing up, William was a happy, pleasant child. But in school, his teachers thought he was **unruly**. School bored William. He wanted more adventure!

So in 1872, William and a friend ran away from home. They went to New York City, New York. There, the boys lived on the streets. To earn money, William sold newspapers. He slept outside on a park bench. The big city was a rough place for a young boy on his own. So after a few weeks, William went home.

Back in Philadelphia, William's parents expected him to attend school. Yet before long, William got into trouble. He liked to pull pranks. One day, he threw a pie at the sign over the school's main entrance. School authorities sent William home and said he could not return.

William's father told him that if he did not go to school, he had to work. But William would not get to sell soap again. Instead, he would make soap in the soap factory. William had to stir large pots of boiling soap for ten hours a day. He earned just $1.50 per week.

During the 1800s, many boys sold newspapers for a living.
They were known as newsboys or newsies.

Soap Salesman

Making soap was hard work. William did not like it very much. He wanted to sell things instead. He had liked selling newspapers in New York City. He had also liked selling soap in Philadelphia. William begged his father to let him work as a salesman.

In 1874, William's father finally agreed. William happily traveled around Pennsylvania and New York. He was a great salesman. William was always polite and friendly to his customers. He listened to them to find out what they wanted. And, William was always persistent. He impressed his father by selling a lot of soap.

When William was 18, he wanted to see if he could make a living on his own. He traveled west and found work as

Wrigley's Mineral Scouring Soap

To sell soap, William traveled long distances in a wagon pulled by horses.

a waiter and a coffee shop cashier. Yet, this was not the life William had imagined. So eventually, he made his way back to Philadelphia and the Wrigley Manufacturing Company.

Starting a Family

William's son, Philip, (right) *and grandson William* (left)

As William grew older, he wanted a family of his own. One day, William met a young lady named Ada Foote. They soon fell in love, and William asked Ada to marry him. She said yes.

The couple married on September 17, 1885. Ada was about 16 when she married William. He was 23 years old. William and Ada wanted to have children. Soon, they had a daughter named Dorothy and a son named Philip.

To support his family, William continued to work for his father's company. Then in 1891, William decided he was ready to start his own business. With just $32 in his pocket, William moved his young family to Chicago, Illinois. There, he would use his sales skills in a whole new way.

William loved Ada dearly.

Perfect Premiums

In Chicago, Wrigley borrowed $5,000 from an uncle. He used the money to start a new company. Wrigley's new business still sold Wrigley's Mineral Scouring Soap. But, he ran the company according to his own ideas.

Wrigley believed everybody enjoyed getting something for nothing. So whenever customers bought soap, Wrigley gave them a premium. At first, this premium was free baking powder.

Just as Wrigley thought, his customers loved the baking powder. In fact, he soon realized they were more interested in it than the soap! So, Wrigley stopped selling soap and sold baking powder instead.

Wrigley still wanted to give his customers a premium. But now, he needed to give away something other than baking powder. In 1892, Wrigley began giving customers two packages of chewing gum. With premiums, Wrigley's business grew.

Wrigley always worked hard to make sure his company was successful.

Big Competition

Wrigley hired the Zeno Gum Company to manufacture his gum. He quickly realized the gum was more popular than the baking powder. So, he decided to stop selling baking powder and only sell gum.

In 1892, Wrigley started a new

At first, gum was wrapped by hand. Today, machines handle this job.

company. He called it Wrigley Chewing Gum. At first, the company sold just a few gum flavors. They were Lotta, Vassar, and Sweet Sixteen Orange. In 1893, Wrigley introduced Juicy Fruit. Later that year, he introduced Spearmint.

Spearmint, Doublemint, and Juicy Fruit are still sold today. P.K. gum is not.

At that time, many companies sold chewing gum. Thomas Adams owned one of the largest gum companies. In 1899, Adams got five other large gum companies to join him. Together, they formed a chewing gum **trust**. The trust became known as the American Chicle Company.

Adams asked Wrigley to add his company to this group. Wrigley said no. He knew he would have trouble competing against such a big company. Still, he wanted to remain independent.

Chew on This

Wrigley had to find a way to increase sales. He focused on the premiums that came with his gum. Wrigley's list of premiums grew.

Wrigley had a talent for knowing how to appeal to his customers.

He gave away lamps, fishing tackle, cookbooks, and more! Customers could choose the premiums they wanted from a catalog.

Wrigley also began offering premiums to store owners that sold his gum. They received cash registers and coffeemakers. This encouraged the store owners to sell a lot of Wrigley's gum.

Most important, Wrigley focused on advertising. He placed ads in magazines and newspapers. He put huge signs on buildings and put billboards along roadways. One row of billboards became

THE BRIGHTEST SPOT ALONG 51
···"THE GREAT WHITE WAY,"
NEW YORK CITY

QUALITY AND FLAVOR
AIDS DIGESTION

WRIGLEY'S SPEARMINT

AFTER EVERY MEAL
THE FLAVOR LASTS

INTERNATIONAL CASINO
DINNER · DANCING · SUPPER

F.W. WOOLWORTH CO

PHOTO BY KEYSTONE

Wrigley believed advertising was the best way to "tell 'em quick and tell 'em often."

famous for its length. It ran along the railroad tracks between Atlantic City and Trenton, New Jersey. People called it the Mile-Long Sign.

Wrigley's advertisements told everyone how great his gum was. This **strategy** made more Americans aware of his product. Advertising and premiums helped Wrigley successfully compete against the American Chicle Company.

Fantastic Flavors

Wrigley's gum has enough brands for everyone to chew their favorite flavor!

Wrigley continued to think of ways to expand his business. He placed gum displays near cash registers in stores. Many shoppers saw the gum and bought it.

Yet, Spearmint gum was not a big seller. Wrigley's solution was to increase advertising. In 1907, he spent almost $250,000 on gum advertisements. That was a fortune in those days! But it was money well spent. Wrigley's gum became more popular. By 1910, Spearmint was the best-selling gum in the United States.

In 1911, Wrigley bought the Zeno factory and established the William Wrigley Jr. Company. From then on, Wrigley's company made all its own products. Wrigley always made sure his products were the best. He said, "Even in a little thing like a stick of gum, quality is important."

In 1914, Wrigley introduced Doublemint. The gum got its name because its mint flavor was double **distilled**. This made the mint double strength. Doublemint is still famous today.

Play Ball!

Wrigley's hard work had paid off. He had become the biggest gum manufacturer in the world. With this success came much wealth. Wrigley decided to spend his money on things he liked.

All his life, Wrigley had loved baseball. So in January 1916, he became a partial owner of the Chicago Cubs baseball team. In 1921, Wrigley became the sole owner. Wrigley loved to attend ball games. He even went on road trips with the team. He hardly ever missed a Cubs game!

The ballpark in Chicago where the Cubs played was renamed Wrigley Field in 1926. Wrigley wanted more fans to come watch the Cubs play. So, he added more bleachers and box seats. He also built an upper deck. These improvements made Wrigley Field a great place for many people to enjoy baseball.

The Chicago Cubs responded positively to Wrigley's good management. They won **National League** championships in 1929, 1932, 1935, and 1938. The Wrigley family owned the Chicago Cubs until 1981.

Wrigley applied the same determination to his baseball team as he had to his business.

Island Escape

The city of Avalon is home to Wrigley's famous Catalina Casino.

In 1919, Wrigley had purchased Santa Catalina Island off the coast of Southern California. He spent much money to add electricity and plumbing on the island. He also built roads, a hotel, and an entertainment building called the Catalina Casino.

The Wrigleys built a lovely home nearby. It sat on a hill that Wrigley named Mount Ada after his wife. Mrs. Wrigley had a huge garden planted on the island. It still grows, featuring plants from all over the world.

In addition, Wrigley built a baseball field on Catalina. In 1921, he brought the Chicago Cubs to the island for their spring training. The Cubs players thought Catalina was beautiful. But,

The Chicago Cubs came to train on Santa Catalina Island almost every year until 1951.

they did not like running up and down all of the island's rugged hills!

Wrigley enjoyed having the Cubs on his island. He watched most of the team's training and games there. He also hosted parties, fishing trips, and other events for team members and their families.

Many reporters came to Catalina to watch spring training. They wrote stories about the Cubs and the beautiful island. Many people who heard the stories wanted to visit the island. It quickly became a popular vacation spot.

Chicago Landmark

Back in Chicago, the William Wrigley Jr. Company continued to do well. Wrigley decided it was time to build an impressive company headquarters downtown. The land Wrigley bought for his new building is **unique** because it is shaped like a triangle. It rests on the north bank of the Chicago River and the northwest corner of Michigan Avenue.

The Wrigley Building is actually two buildings. The south building was completed in April 1921. The north building was completed in May 1924. Walkways called sky bridges connect the buildings.

Construction on the Wrigley Building began in 1920.

On the south building, a large tower stands tall enough to be seen from blocks away. The tower is faced with a clock on all four sides. It was inspired by the Giralda Tower on the Seville Cathedral in Spain. Today, the Wrigley Building is one of the most famous buildings in Chicago. It remains an important landmark there.

The Wrigley Building remains one of Chicago's most beautiful buildings.

Values and Vision

In 2005, the Wrigley Global Innovation Center opened. The laboratories there work to improve the company's products.

By 1925, the Wrigley company had factories in the United States, Canada, and Australia. Wrigley had accomplished much and was ready to retire. He gave his son, Philip, control of the company. Wrigley continued to serve as chairman of the **board**.

Wrigley remained interested in business. In 1930, he became the owner of the Biltmore Hotel in Phoenix, Arizona. He and Mrs. Wrigley enjoyed spending time there. They also continued spending their summers on Catalina. In 1932, the Wrigleys were in Phoenix when Wrigley became very sick. He suffered from heart trouble. William Wrigley Jr. died on January 26.

After his death, Wrigley's family continued to run his company. In 1972, the family formed the Catalina Island Conservancy. It protects the island for the public's enjoyment. The Wrigley family gave much of the island to the conservancy on February 15, 1975.

In 2008, the William Wrigley Jr. Company was purchased by another family-run food company, Mars Inc. Today, customers around the world still enjoy Wrigley's famous brands. The company's products are sold in more than 180 countries.

William Wrigley Jr. did not invent chewing gum, but his company brought it to the world. He was a great salesman. And, he had the vision to use advertising to outsell competitors. Today, businesses everywhere depend on this **strategy** to sell their products.

Timeline

1861	On September 30, William Wrigley Jr. was born in Philadelphia, Pennsylvania.
1874	William became a traveling salesman with the Wrigley Manufacturing Company.
1885	On September 17, William married Ada Foote.
1891	William moved his family to Chicago, Illinois.
1892	Wrigley started a new company called Wrigley Chewing Gum.
1911	Wrigley bought the Zeno Gum Company's factory and established the William Wrigley Jr. Company.
1919	Wrigley bought Santa Catalina Island off the coast of Southern California.
1921	Wrigley became the sole owner of the Chicago Cubs baseball team; Wrigley began bringing the Cubs to Catalina for spring training.
1924	The Wrigley Building was completed in May.
1925	Wrigley retired and gave his son control of the William Wrigley Jr. Company.
1932	On January 26, William Wrigley Jr. died in Phoenix, Arizona.

More to Chew

The William Wrigley Jr. Company has created many different gums over the years. Have you ever chewed any of these brands?

Big Red was introduced in 1976 as Wrigley's first cinnamon gum. It has been the most popular cinnamon gum since 1987. In 2001, the taste of Big Red was updated to offer longer-lasting fresh breath.

Sugar-free gum entered the U.S. market in the late 1970s, but it lacked a great taste. In 1984, Wrigley introduced Extra, which had long-lasting flavor. Within five years, Extra became the best-selling brand of sugar-free gum.

In 1994, Winterfresh created an "icy cool" craze with its unique name and taste.

Orbit was introduced in the United States in 2001. It was originally created in 1944.

In 2007, 5 gum made its U.S. debut. The gum delivers long-lasting flavor and different chewing sensations from each flavor.

Glossary

board - a group of people who manage, direct, or investigate.

distill - to make a liquid or other substance pure by heating and cooling it.

National League - one of the two major leagues in Major League Baseball.

strategy - a careful plan or method.

trust - a group of companies joined by legal agreements. A trust stops competition over a good or a service.

unique - being the only one of its kind.

unruly - not yielding easily to rule or restriction.

Websites

To learn more about Food Dudes,
visit **booklinks.abdopublishing.com**. These links are routinely monitored
and updated to provide the most current information available.

Index